Test Talk
Practice Book

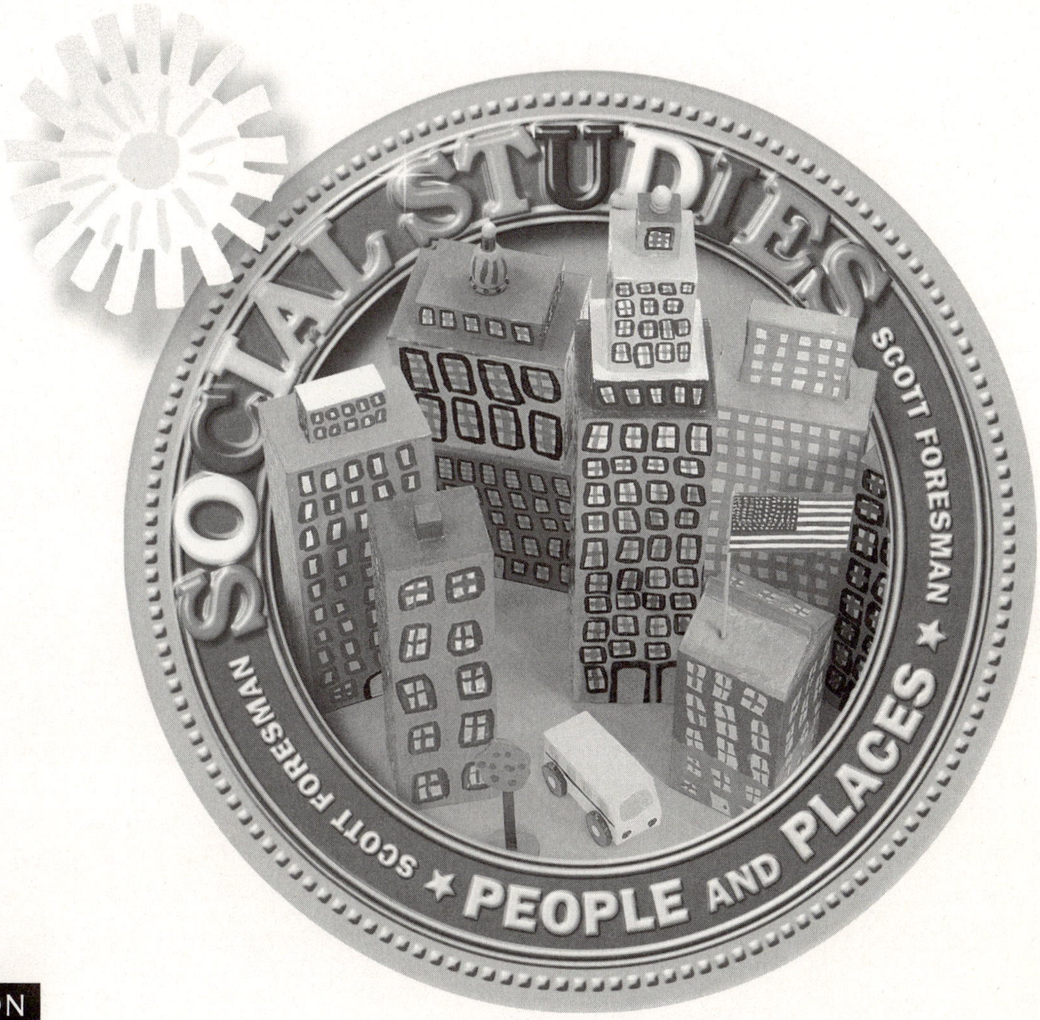

PEARSON
Scott Foresman

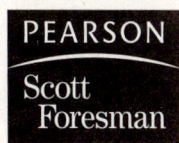

Editorial Offices: Glenview, Illinois • Parsippany, New Jersey • New York, New York
Sales Offices: Parsippany, New Jersey • Duluth, Georgia • Glenview, Illinois • Coppell, Texas • Ontario, California

www.sfsocialstudies.com

ISBN 0-328-04108-4

Copyright © Pearson Education, Inc.
All Rights Reserved. Printed in the United States of America. The publication, or parts thereof, may be used with appropriate equipment to reproduce copies for classroom use only.

16 17 18 19-V0N4-14 13 12 11

Contents

Unit 1

Unit 1 Passage 1
Locate Key Words in the Question 2
Locate Key Words in the Text 3
Choose the Right Answer 4
Use Information from the Text 5
Use Information from Graphics.............. 6
Write Your Answer to Score High 7

Unit 2

Unit 2 Passage..................................... 8
Locate Key Words in the Question.......... 9
Locate Key Words in the Text 10
Choose the Right Answer 11
Use Information from the Text 12
Use Information from Graphics 13
Write Your Answer to Score High 14

Unit 3

Unit 3 Passage..................................... 15
Locate Key Words in the Question.......... 16
Locate Key Words in the Text 17
Choose the Right Answer 18
Use Information from the Text 19
Use Information from Graphics.............. 20
Write Your Answer to Score High 21

Unit 4

Unit 4 Passage 22
Locate Key Words in the Question 23
Locate Key Words in the Text 24
Choose the Right Answer 25
Use Information from the Text 26
Use Information from Graphics 27
Write Your Answer to Score High 28

Unit 5

Unit 5 Passage 29
Locate Key Words in the Question 30
Locate Key Words in the Text 31
Choose the Right Answer 32
Use Information from the Text 33
Use Information from Graphics 34
Write Your Answer to Score High.......... 35

Unit 6

Unit 6 Passage 36
Locate Key Words in the Question 37
Locate Key Words in the Text............... 38
Choose the Right Answer 39
Use Information from the Text 40
Use Information from Graphics 41
Write Your Answer to Score High.......... 42

Where We Live

Directions: Read together.

Kids Care Clubs

Kids Care Clubs first began when a group of children decided to rake a lawn for a neighbor who was old. Later, these children made lunches to give to a soup kitchen. The children felt good because they were able to help neighbors in need.

Today, more than 25,000 children are part of Kids Care Clubs in the United States and Canada. These children have learned how important it is to help others.

Children in Kids Care Clubs show they care by working on special projects. Some clubs collected food, toys, and blankets for people who lost their homes in an earthquake. One club made bedtime snacks for children in a homeless shelter.

Name _____

Test Talk

Use with Unit 1.

Strategy 1 — Locate Key Words in the Question

Learn

Circle key words. Tell what you need to find out.

1. (How) did (Kids Care Clubs) first (begin)?

   I need to find out how Kids Care Clubs first began. _____
   _____
   _____

Try It

2. How many children are part of Kids Care Clubs in the United States and Canada?

   I need to find out _____
   _____
   _____

3. What was collected for people who lost their homes in an earthquake?

   I need to find out _____
   _____
   _____

  Have students: • Read the question. • Circle key words in the question.
• Think: "I need to find out…"

Name _____

Test Talk
Use with Unit 1.

Strategy 2 **Locate Key Words in the Text**

Learn

Circle key words in the question. Circle key words in the text.

1. (How) did (Kids Care Clubs) first (begin)?

   The key words in the text are Kids Care Clubs, began, group,

   rake, and lawn.

Try It

2. How many children are part of Kids Care Clubs in the United States and Canada?

   The key words in the text are _____

3. What was collected for people who lost their homes in an earthquake?

   The key words in the text are _____

Have students: • Read the question. • Circle key words in the question.
• Circle key words in the text. • Finish the sentence: "The key words in the text are…"

Test Talk Practice Book   Unit 1 **3**

Name _____

Test Talk

Use with Unit 1.

Strategy 3 Choose the Right Answer

Learn

Choose the best answer.

1. How did Kids Care Clubs first begin?
   - ~~when a school in Connecticut thought it was a good idea~~
   - ~~when people lost their homes after an earthquake~~
   - ● when a group of children decided to rake a lawn for a neighbor
   - ~~when people needed help after a blizzard~~

Try It

2. How many children are part of Kids Care Clubs in the United States and Canada?
   - ○ 5,000
   - ○ more than 25,000
   - ○ just over 250
   - ○ 500

3. What was collected for people who lost their homes in an earthquake?
   - ○ sticks and stones
   - ○ money
   - ○ food, toys, and blankets
   - ○ wood and bricks

© Scott Foresman 2

 Have students: • Read the question. • Read all the answer choices. • Rule out any incorrect choices. • Mark the best answer choice.

4 Unit 1

Test Talk Practice Book

Name _____

Test Talk
Use with Unit 1.

Strategy 4 — Use Information from the Text

Learn

Circle key words in the question. Circle key words in the text. Answer the question.

1. (How) did (Kids Care Clubs) first (begin)?

   Kids Care Clubs first began when children raked a lawn for a

   neighbor who was old.

   _____

Try It

2. How many children are part of Kids Care Clubs in the United States and Canada?

   _____
   _____
   _____

3. What was collected for people who lost their homes in an earthquake?

   _____
   _____
   _____

Have students: • Read the question. • Circle key words in the question.
• Circle key words in the text. • Use details from the text to answer the question.

Test Talk Practice Book — Unit 1 **5**

Name _____

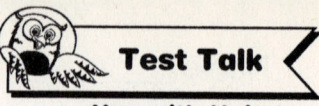

Test Talk
Use with Unit 1.

Strategy 5 **Use Information from Graphics**

Learn

Circle key words in the question. Use the photograph on page 1 to answer the question.

1. (What) would (help) (children) who do (not) (have) (toys)?
   The teddy bear and ball would help children who do not have toys.
   _____
   _____

Try It

2. What would help people who need to eat?
   _____
   _____
   _____

3. What would help people who are cold?
   _____
   _____
   _____

 Have students: • Read the question. • Circle key words in the question.
• Use details from the photograph to answer the question.

6 Unit 1

Test Talk Practice Book

Name _____

Test Talk
Use with Unit 1.

Strategy 6 Write Your Answer to Score High

Learn

Look at this example.

1. (How) did (Kids Care Clubs) first (begin)?

   Kids Care Clubs first began when children raked a lawn for a

   neighbor. Later, they made lunches for a soup kitchen.

   Is the answer correct?
   Is the answer complete?
   Do all the details help answer the question?
   What should you do to improve the answer?

Try It

Circle key words in each question. Write an answer.

2. What made the children feel good?

   _____

   _____

3. How do children in Kids Care Clubs show they care?

   _____

   _____

   _____

 Have students: • Read the question. • Circle key words in the question. • Use details from the text to write an answer. • Ask: "Is the answer correct? Is the answer complete? Do all the details help answer the question?"

Test Talk Practice Book   Unit 1 **7**

Our Earth

Directions: Read together.

How and Where People Lived

Native Americans, also known as American Indians, were the first people to live in what is now the United States. They used land, water, plants, and animals to meet their needs. A need is something people must have to live.

Native Americans lived in areas with different climates. They used things found in nature to make their homes.

Many groups of Native Americans lived in an area called the Great Plains. These Native Americans were called Plains Indians. Some Plains Indians were farmers. They planned their lives around the changing seasons. Spring was the time to plant. Fall was the time to harvest.

Many Plains Indians hunted animals for food. They used animal skins to keep warm. Some lived in a kind of tent called a tepee.

Name _____

Test Talk
Use with Unit 2.

Strategy 1 **Locate Key Words in the Question**

Learn

Circle key words. Tell what you need to find out.

1. (Who) were the (first) (people) to live in what is now the (United States)?

   I need to find out <u>who the first people to live in the United</u>

   <u>States were.</u>

Try It

2. What did Native Americans use to make their homes?

   I need to find out _____

   _____

   _____

3. Where did many groups of Native Americans live?

   I need to find out _____

   _____

   _____

Have students: • Read the question. • Circle key words in the question.
• Think: "I need to find out…"

Test Talk Practice Book

Name _____

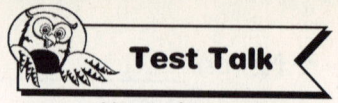

Strategy 2 **Locate Key Words in the Text**

Learn

Circle key words in the question. Circle key words in the text.

1. (Who) were the (first) (people) to live in what is now the (United States)?

    The key words in the text are Native Americans, first, people,

    and United States.

Try It

2. What did Native Americans use to make their homes?

    The key words in the text are _____

3. Where did many groups of Native Americans live?

    The key words in the text are _____

Have students: • Read the question. • Circle key words in the question.
• Circle key words in the text. • Finish the sentence: "The key words in the text are…"

Name _____

Test Talk
Use with Unit 2.

Strategy 3 Choose the Right Answer

Learn

Choose the best answer.

1. Who were the first people to live in what is now the United States?
   - ~~Europeans~~
   - ~~Mexicans~~
   - ~~Vikings~~
   - ● Native Americans

Try It

2. Where did many groups of Native Americans live?
   - ○ Great Plains
   - ○ cities
   - ○ Europe
   - ○ towns

3. What season was the time to plant?
   - ○ summer
   - ○ fall
   - ○ winter
   - ○ spring

Have students: • Read the question. • Read all the answer choices.
• Rule out any incorrect choices. • Mark the best answer choice.

Test Talk Practice Book   Unit 2 **11**

Name _____

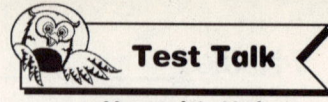

Use with Unit 2.

Strategy 4 Use Information from the Text

Learn

Circle key words in the question. Circle key words in the text. Answer the question.

1. (What) is a (need)?

   A need is something people must have to live.
   _____
   _____

Try It

2. Based on the passage, where did many Native Americans live?

   _____
   _____
   _____

3. What did Plains Indians who were farmers plan their lives around?

   _____
   _____
   _____

 Have students: • Read the question. • Circle key words in the question.
• Circle key words in the text. • Use details from the text to answer the question.

12 Unit 2   Test Talk Practice Book

Name _____

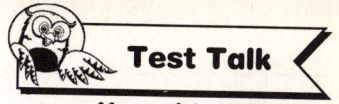
Test Talk
Use with Unit 2.

Strategy 5 — Use Information from Graphics

Learn

Circle key words in the question. Use the picture on page 8 to answer the question.

1. (What) (shape) are the (tepees), or Native American tents?

   The tepees are shaped like triangles.
   _____

Try It

2. Based on the picture, what did the Native Americans use for transportation?

   _____
   _____
   _____

3. How do the tepees meet the needs of American Indians?

   _____
   _____
   _____
   _____

 Have students: • Read the question. • Circle key words in the question.
• Use details from the picture to answer the question.

Test Talk Practice Book   Unit 2   **13**

Name _____

Test Talk
Use with Unit 2.

Strategy 6 **Write Your Answer to Score High**

Learn

Look at this example.

1. (What) is a (need)?

   A need is something that people want to make their lives better.
   _____

   Is the answer correct?
   Is the answer complete?
   Do all the details help answer the question?
   What should you do to improve the answer?

Try It

Circle key words in each question. Write an answer.

2. What did Native Americans use to make their homes?

   _____
   _____

3. Why did some Plains Indians hunt animals?

   _____
   _____
   _____

 Have students: • Read the question. • Circle key words in the question. • Use details from the text to write an answer. • Ask: "Is the answer correct? Is the answer complete? Do all the details help answer the question?"

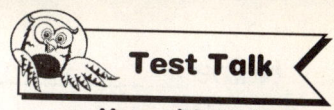

Working Together

Directions: Read together.

Meet Florence Nightingale

1820–1910, Hospital Reformer and Nurse

Florence Nightingale was a famous nurse. She spent her life serving and caring for others.

Long ago, Florence Nightingale was a leader of nurses. She was in charge of caring for army soldiers during a war. When she arrived at the army hospital, she found it too crowded. The soldiers' clothing was dirty. There were not enough beds.

Florence Nightingale was determined to give the soldiers the best care possible. She bought supplies. She worked day and night at the army hospital to care for the soldiers.

After the war, Florence Nightingale started the world's first school of nursing. She wanted nurses to be educated and trained properly.

Florence Nightingale at work in a hospital.

Name _____

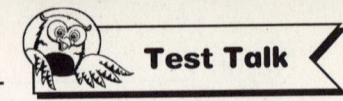

Use with Unit 3.

Strategy 1 Locate Key Words in the Question

Learn

Circle key words. Tell what you need to find out.

1. (Who) was Florence (Nightingale) in (charge) of (caring) for?

   I need to find out _who Florence Nightingale was in charge of_

   caring for. _____

   _____

Try It

2. What was Florence Nightingale determined to give the soldiers?

   I need to find out _____

   _____

   _____

3. Why did Florence Nightingale start a school of nursing?

   I need to find out _____

   _____

   _____

Have students: • Read the question. • Circle key words in the question.
• Think: "I need to find out…"

Unit 3   Test Talk Practice Book

Name _____

Test Talk
Use with Unit 3.

Strategy 2 Locate Key Words in the Text

Learn

Circle key words in the question. Circle key words in the text.

1. (Who) was Florence (Nightingale) in (charge) of (caring) for?

   The key words in the text are charge, caring, army, and

   soldiers.

Try It

2. What was Florence Nightingale determined to give the soldiers?

   The key words in the text are _____

   _____

   _____

3. Why did Florence Nightingale start a school of nursing?

   The key words in the text are _____

   _____

   _____

 Have students: • Read the question. • Circle key words in the question.
• Circle key words in the text. • Finish the sentence: "The key words in the text are..."

Test Talk Practice Book   Unit 3 **17**

Name _____

Test Talk
Use with Unit 3.

Strategy 3   Choose the Right Answer

Learn

Choose the best answer.

1. Who was Florence Nightingale in charge of caring for?

   ● army soldiers
   ○ ~~birds that sing at night~~
   ○ ~~hotel guests~~
   ○ ~~doctors~~

Try It

2. What was Florence Nightingale determined to give the soldiers?

   ○ education
   ○ proper training
   ○ guns and ammunition
   ○ the best care possible

3. Why did Florence Nightingale start a school of nursing?

   ○ to give soldiers the best possible care
   ○ to educate and train nurses
   ○ to make a lot of money
   ○ to stop wars

Have students: • Read the question. • Read all the answer choices.
• Rule out any incorrect choices. • Mark the best answer choice.

18   Unit 3   Test Talk Practice Book

Name _____

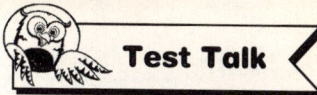

Use with Unit 3.

Strategy 4 — Use Information from the Text

Learn

Circle key words in the question. Circle key words in the text. Answer the question.

1. (Who) was Florence (Nightingale) in (charge) of (caring) for?

   Florence Nightingale was in charge of caring for army soldiers

   during a war.

Try It

2. What was Florence Nightingale determined to give the soldiers?

   _____

   _____

   _____

3. What did Florence Nightingale start after the war?

   _____

   _____

   _____

   _____

 Have students: • Read the question. • Circle key words in the question.
• Circle key words in the text. • Use details from the text to answer the question.

Test Talk Practice Book   Unit 3 **19**

Name _____

Test Talk
Use with Unit 3.

Strategy 5 Use Information from Graphics

Learn

Circle key words in the question. Use the picture on page 15 to answer the question.

1. (What) is the (job) of the (women) in the picture?

   The women are nurses. _____
   _____

Try It

2. Who might the men in the picture be?

   _____
   _____
   _____

3. Where is Florence Nightingale working in the picture?

   _____
   _____
   _____
   _____

Have students: • Read the question. • Circle key words in the question.
• Use details from the picture to answer the question.

20   Unit 3   Test Talk Practice Book

Name _____

Test Talk

Use with Unit 3.

Strategy 6 Write Your Answer to Score High

Learn

Look at this example.

1. (What) did Florence (Nightingale) (start) after the war?

   Florence Nightingale started a school for teachers. _____

   Is the answer correct?
   Is the answer complete?
   Do all the details help answer the question?
   What should you do to improve the answer?

Try It

Circle key words in each question. Write an answer.

2. What was the soldiers' clothing like at the army hospital?

   _____

   _____

3. Why did Florence Nightingale start a school of nursing?

   _____

   _____

 Have students: • Read the question. • Circle key words in the question. • Use details from the text to write an answer. • Ask: "Is the answer correct? Is the answer complete? Do all the details help answer the question?"

Test Talk Practice Book

Unit 3 **21**

Our Country Today

Directions: Read together.

Meet Thurgood Marshall

1908–1993, Supreme Court Justice

Thurgood Marshall was the first African American justice on the Supreme Court.

When Thurgood was a young boy, his father would take him to the courthouse to watch trials. When Thurgood was older he applied to law school but was turned down because he was an African American. This event led him to spend the rest of his life working for equal rights. He was accepted at another law school, where he graduated at the top of his class.

As a lawyer, Thurgood Marshall brought many cases before the Supreme Court. In one case, black children could not go to school with white children. Thurgood Marshall won this case. Later, Thurgood Marshall was chosen to become a Supreme Court Justice.

Supreme Court Justices, 1967

Name _____

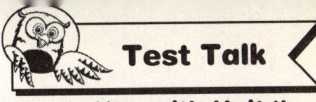

Test Talk

Use with Unit 4.

Strategy 1 **Locate Key Words in the Question**

Learn

Circle key words. Tell what you need to find out.

1. (Who) was Thurgood (Marshall)?

   I need to find out <u>who Thurgood Marshall was.</u>

   _____

   _____

Try It

2. Why was Thurgood Marshall turned down by law school?

   I need to find out _____

   _____

   _____

3. How did being turned down by law school change Thurgood Marshall's life?

   I need to find out _____

   _____

   _____

 Have students: • Read the question. • Circle key words in the question.
• Think: "I need to find out…"

Test Talk Practice Book

Unit 4 **23**

Name _____

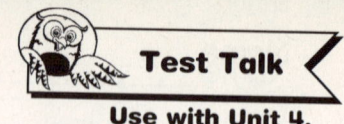

Use with Unit 4.

Strategy 2 Locate Key Words in the Text

Learn

Circle key words in the question. Circle key words in the text.

1. (Who) was Thurgood (Marshall)?

    The key words in the text are Marshall, first, African American, justice, Supreme, and Court.

Try It

2. Why was Thurgood Marshall turned down by law school at first?

    The key words in the text are _____

3. How did being turned down by law school change Thurgood Marshall's life?

    The key words in the text are _____

 Have students: • Read the question. • Circle key words in the question.
• Circle key words in the text. • Finish the sentence: "The key words in the text are..."

24 Unit 4

Test Talk Practice Book

Name _____

Test Talk
Use with Unit 4.

Strategy 3 **Choose the Right Answer**

Learn

Choose the best answer.

1. Who was Thurgood Marshall?
   ○ ~~a famous baseball player~~
   ○ ~~a sheriff in the Wild West~~
   ● a Supreme Court justice
   ○ ~~a famous wrestler~~

Try It

2. Why was Thurgood Marshall turned down by law school at first?
   ○ because he was an African American
   ○ because he wanted his brother to go to the school
   ○ because his grades were too low
   ○ because the school did not have any more room

3. Where did Thurgood Marshall bring many of his law cases?
   ○ to the courtyard
   ○ before the Supreme Court
   ○ before the Pennsylvania Court
   ○ before the court of justice

 Have students: • Read the question. • Read all the answer choices.
• Rule out any incorrect choices. • Mark the best answer choice.

Test Talk Practice Book

Unit 4   **25**

Name _____

Test Talk
Use with Unit 4.

Strategy 4 — Use Information from the Text

Learn

Circle key words in the question. Circle key words in the text. Answer the question.

1. (Who) was Thurgood (Marshall)?

   Thurgood Marshall was the first African American justice on the Supreme Court.

Try It

2. Why was Thurgood Marshall turned down by law school at first?

3. How did being turned down by law school change Thurgood Marshall's life?

Have students: • Read the question. • Circle key words in the question. • Circle key words in the text. • Use details from the text to answer the question.

Name _____

Test Talk
Use with Unit 4.

Strategy 5 Use Information from Graphics

Learn

Circle key words in the question. Use the photograph on page 22 to answer the question.

1. (How) (many) (justices) are on the Supreme Court?

   There are nine justices on the Supreme Court.

Try It

2. In what year was this photograph taken?

3. How many of the Supreme Court justices were women in 1967?

Have students: • Read the question. • Circle key words in the question.
• Use details from the photograph to answer the question.

Test Talk Practice Book

Unit 4

Name _____

Test Talk
Use with Unit 4.

Strategy 6 — Write Your Answer to Score High

Learn

Look at this example.

1. (How) did Thurgood's (father) (influence) his (life)?

   Thurgood's father influenced his life by taking him to court.
   _____

   Is the answer correct?
   Is the answer complete?
   Do all the details help answer the question?
   What should you do to improve the answer?

Try It

Circle key words in each question. Write an answer.

2. Where did Thurgood Marshall graduate in his class in law school?

   _____
   _____

3. What was the problem in one case Thurgood Marshall brought before the Supreme Court?

   _____
   _____
   _____

 Have students: • Read the question. • Circle key words in the question. • Use details from the text to write an answer. • Ask: "Is the answer correct? Is the answer complete? Do all the details help answer the question?"

Name _____

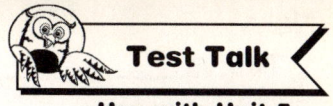

Use with Unit 5.

Our Country Long Ago

Directions: Read together.

Westward Ho!

Many people wanted to come to the West. Trains were a faster way to travel than covered wagons. Trains were needed so that communities in the West could get the supplies they needed.

There were many railroads in the East, but few in the West. The country needed a railroad that could link the East Coast to the West Coast.

Two groups built the western part of the railroad. One group started near Omaha, Nebraska. The other group started in Sacramento, California. The two groups met and joined the railroad tracks at Promontory Point in present-day Utah. It took seven years to build this railroad.

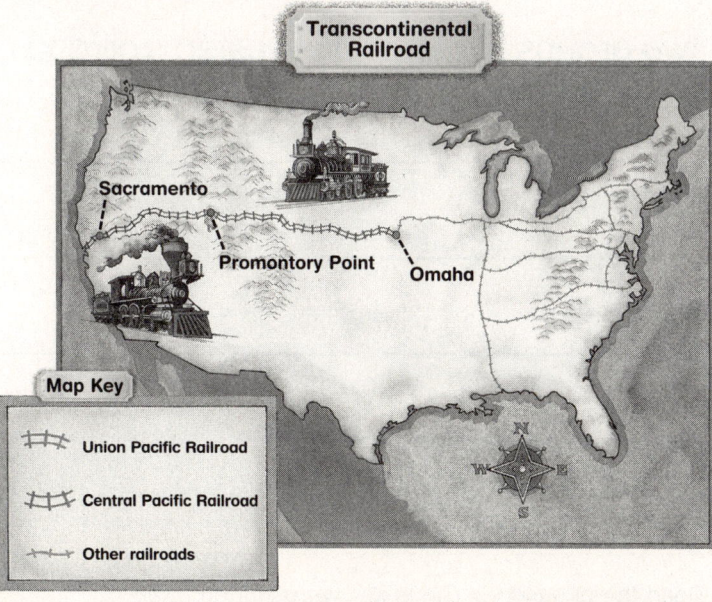

Test Talk Practice Book Unit 5 **29**

Name _____

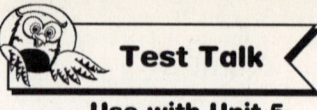

Use with Unit 5.

Strategy 1 **Locate Key Words in the Question**

Learn

Circle key words. Tell what you need to find out.

1. (Why) did (people) already in the (West) (need) (trains)?

    I need to find out why people already in the West needed trains. _____

Try It

2. What kind of railroad did the country need?

    I need to find out _____

3. Where did the two groups that built the western railroad meet?

    I need to find out _____

Have students: • Read the question. • Circle key words in the question.
• Think: "I need to find out…"

30 Unit 5 Test Talk Practice Book

Name _____

Test Talk
Use with Unit 5.

Strategy 2 Locate Key Words in the Text

Learn

Circle key words in the question. Circle key words in the text.

1. (Why) did (people) already in the (West) (need) (trains)?

   The key words in the text are trains, needed, West, and

   supplies.

   _____

Try It

2. What kind of railroad did the country need?

   The key words in the text are _____

   _____

   _____

3. Where did the two groups that built the western railroad meet?

   The key words in the text are _____

   _____

   _____

Have students: • Read the question. • Circle key words in the question.
• Circle key words in the text. • Finish the sentence: "The key words in the text are..."

Test Talk Practice Book   Unit 5 **31**

Name _____

Test Talk

Use with Unit 5.

Strategy 3   Choose the Right Answer

Learn

Choose the best answer.

1. Why did people already in the West need trains?

   ○ ~~so they could go live in the East~~
   ● so they could get supplies
   ○ ~~so they could provide supplies to people in the East~~
   ○ ~~so they could meet people in the East~~

Try It

2. What kind of railroad did the country need?

   ○ one that traveled into the rain forest
   ○ one that could link the North to the South
   ○ one that was more comfortable
   ○ one that could link the East Coast to the West Coast

3. Where did the two groups that built the western railroad meet?

   ○ Omaha, Nebraska
   ○ Sacramento, California
   ○ Promontory Point in present-day Utah
   ○ on the West Coast

 Have students: • Read the question. • Read all the answer choices.
• Rule out any incorrect choices. • Mark the best answer choice.

32   Unit 5   Test Talk Practice Book

Name _____

Test Talk
Use with Unit 5.

Strategy 4 **Use Information from the Text**

Learn

Circle key words in the question. Circle key words in the text. Answer the question.

1. (Why) did (people) already in the (West) (need) (trains)?

   People in the West needed trains to get supplies.
   _____
   _____

Try It

2. What kind of railroad did the country need?
   _____
   _____
   _____

3. Where did the two groups that built the western railroad meet?
   _____
   _____
   _____

Have students: • Read the question. • Circle key words in the question.
• Circle key words in the text. • Use details from the text to answer the question.

Test Talk Practice Book
Unit 5

Name _____

Test Talk
Use with Unit 5.

Strategy 5 — Use Information from Graphics

Learn

Circle key words in the question. Use the map on page 29 to answer the question.

1. (What) (two) (railroads) are named in the map key?

   The two railroads named in the map key are the Union Pacific

   Railroad and the Central Pacific Railroad.

   _____

Try It

2. What directions do the two railroads go?

   _____

   _____

   _____

3. Is Promontory Point east or west of Omaha?

   _____

   _____

   _____

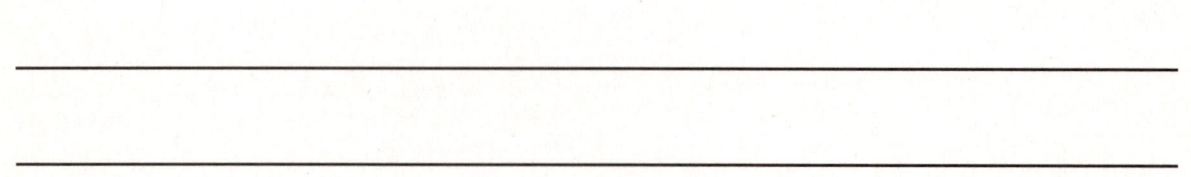

 Have students: • Read the question. • Circle key words in the question.
• Use details from the map to answer the question.

34 Unit 5   Test Talk Practice Book

Name _____

Test Talk

Use with Unit 5.

Strategy 6 Write Your Answer to Score High

Learn

Look at this example.

1. (How) did (trains) (help) (communities) in the (West)?

   Trains helped communities in the West travel faster than covered wagons.

   Is the answer correct?
   Is the answer complete?
   Do all the details help answer the question?
   What should you do to improve the answer?

Try It

Circle key words in each question. Write an answer.

2. How many groups built the western part of the railroad?

   _____

   _____

3. How long did it take to build the western part of the railroad?

   _____

   _____

 Have students: • Read the question. • Circle key words in the question. • Use details from the text to write an answer. • Ask: "Is the answer correct? Is the answer complete? Do all the details help answer the question?"

Test Talk Practice Book　　　　　　　　　　　　　　　　　　　Unit 5　**35**

People and Places in History

Directions: Read together.

Landmarks Around the World

The Great Wall of China was built more than 2,000 years ago. It took about one million people to build it! Ancient Chinese states first built walls for protection. Later these walls were joined together and called the Great Wall.

If you put the Great Wall across the United States, from east to west, it would be much longer than our country!

Name _____

Test Talk

Use with Unit 6.

Strategy 1 **Locate Key Words in the Question**

Learn

Circle key words. Tell what you need to find out.

1. (When) was the (Great Wall) of China (built)?

   I need to find out <u>when the Great Wall of China was built.</u>
   _____
   _____

Try It

2. How many people did it take to build the Great Wall?

   I need to find out _____
   _____
   _____

3. Why did the ancient Chinese states first build walls?

   I need to find out _____
   _____
   _____

Have students: • Read the question. • Circle key words in the question.
• Think: "I need to find out…"

Test Talk Practice Book   Unit 6 **37**

Name _____

Test Talk
Use with Unit 6.

Strategy 2 **Locate Key Words in the Text**

Learn

Circle key words in the question. Circle key words in the text.

1. (When) was the (Great Wall) of China (built)?

    The key words in the text are Great Wall, built, more, than,

    2,000, and years.

    _____

Try It

2. How many people did it take to build the Great Wall?

    The key words in the text are _____

    _____

    _____

3. Why did the ancient Chinese states first build walls?

    The key words in the text are _____

    _____

    _____

Have students: • Read the question. • Circle key words in the question.
• Circle key words in the text. • Finish the sentence: "The key words in the text are…"

38 Unit 6　　　　　　　　　　　　　　　　　　　Test Talk Practice Book

Name _____

Test Talk
Use with Unit 6.

Strategy 3 Choose the Right Answer

Learn

Choose the best answer.

1. When was the Great Wall of China built?

    ● more than 2,000 years ago
    ○ ~~more than 200 years ago~~
    ○ ~~less than 200 years ago~~
    ○ ~~less than 2,000 years ago~~

Try It

2. How many people did it take to build the Great Wall?

    ○ more than 2,000
    ○ less than 2,000
    ○ about one million
    ○ about two million

3. Why did the ancient Chinese states first build walls?

    ○ to hang posters
    ○ for fun
    ○ for protection
    ○ to honor soldiers

 Have students: • Read the question. • Read all the answer choices.
• Rule out any incorrect choices. • Mark the best answer choice.

Test Talk Practice Book   Unit 6 **39**

Name _____

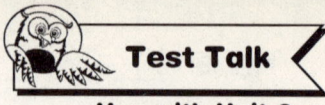

Strategy 4 **Use Information from the Text**

Learn

Circle key words in the question. Circle key words in the text. Answer the question.

1. (When) was the (Great Wall) of China (built)?

   The Great Wall of China was built more than 2,000 years ago.
   _____
   _____

Try It

2. How many people did it take to build the Great Wall?

   _____
   _____
   _____

3. Why did the ancient Chinese states first build walls?

   _____
   _____
   _____

 Have students: • Read the question. • Circle key words in the question.
• Circle key words in the text. • Use details from the text to answer the question.

40 Unit 6 Test Talk Practice Book

Name _____

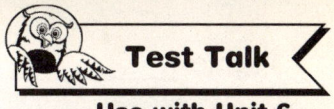

Test Talk

Use with Unit 6.

Strategy 5 Use Information from Graphics

Learn

Circle key words in the question. Use the photograph on page 36 to answer the question.

1. (What) is (shown) in the photograph?

   The Great Wall of China is shown in the photograph.
   _____
   _____

Try It

2. What is one of the natural resources shown in the photograph?

   _____
   _____
   _____

3. Does the Great Wall have curves or is it straight?

   _____
   _____
   _____

Have students: • Read the question. • Circle key words in the question.
• Use details from the photograph to answer the question.

Test Talk Practice Book   Unit 6   **41**

Name _____

Test Talk
Use with Unit 6.

Strategy 6 **Write Your Answer to Score High**

Learn

Look at this example.

1. (When) was the (Great Wall) of China (built)?

   The Great Wall of China was built more than 2,000 years ago.

   About one million people built it.

   Is the answer correct?
   Is the answer complete?
   Do all the details help answer the question?
   What should you do to improve the answer?

Try It

Circle key words in each question. Write an answer.

2. What were the walls called when they were joined together?

   _____

   _____

3. How long is the Great Wall compared with the United States?

   _____

   _____

 Have students: • Read the question. • Circle key words in the question. • Use details from the text to write an answer. • Ask: "Is the answer correct? Is the answer complete? Do all the details help answer the question?"

Acknowledgements

Illustrations

29 Tony Morse

Photographs

Every effort has been made to secure permission and provide appropriate credit for photographic material. The publisher deeply regrets any omission and pledges to correct errors called to their attention in subsequent editions.

Unless otherwise acknowledged, all photographs are the property of Scott Foresman, a division of Pearson Education.

8 Corbis/Corbis-Bettmann
15 Hulton Getty
22 Bettman Archives/Corbis-Bettmann
36 Peter Menzel/Stock Boston